HOME, SWEET HOME

MEMORIES OF TIGER STADIUM

From the archives of

The Detroit News

Published by Sports Publishing Inc.

www.SportsPublishingInc.com

The Detroit News

MARK SILVERMAN, Publisher and Editor | JENNIFER CARROLL, Managing Editor

BOOK CREDITS

STEVE FECHT, Photo Editor

DAVID KORDALSKI, Cover and Book Design

ALAN WHITT, Copy Editor

JEFF SAMORAY, Research

Hardcover: ISBN 1-58261-136-x; Paperback: ISBN 1-58261-137-8

Library of Congress Number: 99-63138

Published by Sports Publishing Inc.
www.SportsPublishingInc.com

Printed in the United States

FOREWORD BY AL KALINE

ust about every summer since I was 18 years old I've had a home at Tiger Stadium. I was there 21½ years as a player, and now through all these years as a broadcaster, it has remained a special part of my life.

It was the closeness of the fans that I'll always remember — the way you could hear people talking in the stands, talking as I stood in the on-deck circle. They might not even be talking to you, but you could hear their conversations so clearly, as if you were sitting next to them.

The upper deck, too, was so close — probably as close as any upper deck in baseball ever was, or ever will be. A player could sense that fans enjoyed a game a little

more at Tiger Stadium — that feeling of people sitting in stands so tight to the field that they could touch you.

I remember playing right field with that upper-deck overhang behind me. Opposing players, left-hand hitters especially, loved coming here. I knew so many players who were injured who wouldn't miss their chance at playing in Detroit. They'd get taped up, wrapped up, just like I would do whatever it took to play in Fenway Park in Boston.

I remember parking my car and walking through the stands, getting to know the concession people and saying hi to all those folks every day.

It will be emotional on that last day at Tiger Stadium. I'm preparing for it. I'm going to feel it more than I want.

Cornerstone of memories

BY GEORGE CANTOR | THE DETROIT NEWS

here is more to a city than wrecking crews can destroy. Much more than mere brick, steel and concrete.

A city is shared memory, an emotional legacy to be passed on from one generation to the next. It is the sound of birds and traffic, the angle at which the sunlight falls on an early spring afternoon, the texture of its daily life that makes one city unlike any other.

That is why this glorious hulk of a ballpark matters. Whether it was called Bennett Park or Navin Field, Briggs

or Tiger Stadium, it came the closest, more than any other single edifice or institution, to defining the soul of Detroit.

Even in our most impoverished, most divided, most hopeless hours, this is where we gathered to be enriched, to unite, to hope.

It will continue to matter long after the Tigers have moved out, long after it is reduced to twisted metal and stone, long after the outfield grass withers and the bleachers collapse and Al Kaline's old locker in the corner of the clubhouse disappears.

Because five generations of Detroiters will see it in their minds, feel its damp in their bones, hold its memories in their heart's deepest core.

AT ONE TIME IT WAS CONSIDERED UNSEEMLY TO ATTEND SUNDAY BASEBALL GAMES. BUT ON AUGUST 18, 1907 THE TIGERS HOSTED THE NEW YORK HIGHLANDERS AT BENNETT PARK AND A NEW ERA ARRIVED.

Listen.

"Scorecards a dime; lineups a dime. C'mon you Tigers. He stood there like the house by the side of the road. I shoulda' stood in bed. Batting cleanup for the Tigers, Number Five, Hank Greenberg. Layne spots Doran down the right sideline....touchdown, and there's bedlam at Briggs Stadium. Bless you, boys. Viva Mandela. Go get 'em, Tigers. How'm I doin', Edna?

"Hold my hand tight when we walk up this ramp, son. Joe, this is a dangerous situation and you're going to have to come out of this game. Didn't ole Diz tell ya me n' Paul would win this thing? Louis is measuring his man, moving in for the kill. The entire front four was in on Starr that time, led by Karras and Roger Brown. He ain't gonna pitch to you, Gibby....And the home of the brave."

The Lions won two NFL championships, the

last one 42 years ago, on this field. There have been title fights, political rallies, concerts, the high school Goodfellow games.

But it was a park built for baseball. Its

dimensions and peculiar corners, its rightfield overhang and roof, its centerfield flagpole right on the playing field, its ghosts and its echoes, all are part of the summer game. No ballpark anywhere is quite the same. That is the source of Tiger Stadium's hold on this city.

This is the field where Ty Cobb's razor-sharp spikes dug into the turf; where Wahoo Sam Crawford and George Kell ripped line drives to the outfield corners; where Prince Hal reigned and Frank Lary stared down the imperious Yankees; where Mickey Stanley ran down another long one to center and Lance Parrish cut down another runner.

Where the history of a sport and the story of a city are intermingled everywhere you look.

"I walked into that stadium last summer for the first time in 30 years and it was like all the years in between had been stripped away," says Tom Huth, a former Detroiter who now lives in Boulder, Colo.

"For those first few minutes, it was like I was back in college and we were going out to see Jake Wood and Billy Bruton. It was eerie, the way it all looked the same, like it had been preserved in a time capsule. It wasn't until about the eighth inning that it started to sink in that this was going to be the last time I'd ever see it."

Other cities lost their old ballparks. Some barely noticed their passing, moving on to new stadiums without so much as a backward glance.

But in others, the hurt still throbs.

In Pittsburgh, they speak longingly of the cozy neighborhood atmosphere of old Forbes Field. In Cincinnati, a farmer from nearby Kentucky salvaged a portion of the Crosley Field grandstand and reassembled it in one of his fields to keep some part of the park alive.

And in Brooklyn, nothing can ever replace Ebbets Field; built in 1912, the same year Navin Field opened on the configuration of the existing Tiger Stadium.

"I hit a home run in Ebbets Field during a high school all star game more than 40 years ago," says Norman Brill, of Oceanside, N.Y. "You know, I still get people when they hear my name ask: 'Aren't you the guy who hit the home run at Ebbets Field?' A few times a year that happens, and the guy always shakes his head and smiles.

"I'm not going to say that was the high point of my life. But to watch that ball going into the seats, with everything that ballpark meant to Brooklyn...yeah, there aren't too many that topped it. So I know what a ballpark can mean to a city, and I know what it's like to lose it."

Only four ballparks from baseball's golden age survive at the century's final year. There is Boston's Fenway Park, Chicago's Wrigley Field, New York's Yankee Stadium and this one. And in both Boston and New York there also is talk of replacement.

All of these ballparks are treasures, a defining part of their communities. But in Detroit, a city that has endured much, the stadium occupies a space that transcends baseball.

At times, when there seemed to be no common ground, there was the turf of this ballpark. And it helped to get us through.

In the Depression, when many Detroiters were hard pressed to come up with trolley fare, they would walk here from across the city and count out their nickels and pennies to buy a grandstand seat.

FANTASTIC FEATS, SUCH AS SCHOOLBOY ROWE'S 16-GAME WINNING STREAK IN 1934, MADE THE DEPRESSION A BIT EASIER FOR TIGER FANS TO DIGEST.

These were people who had lost almost everything; jobs, money, in many cases their homes. The auto industry was running on empty. No city in America was laid lower in the 1930s.

But they came to this field and they saw Schoolboy Rowe winning 16 straight games, and Hank Greenberg slamming another one into the seats, and Charlie Gehringer making the impossible look effortless at second base, and the burning eyes of Mickey Cochrane, goading and driving and willing the Tigers to a pennant. For those old enough to remember, there will never be another time or team quite like it. Because when there seemed to be no hope, in this place they learned how to hope again.

In the spring of 1968, the suspicion and distrust and hatred that had torn the city apart still raged with the intensity of the previous summer's flames. Wild rumors raced through streets still scarred with burned-out homes and stores.

It seemed there was nowhere left to come together, no place to meet or to heal.

Then Denny McLain began to win, and Gates Brown walked off the bench to deliver another clutch hit, and Jim Northrup hit his grand slams and Willie Horton, right off the streets of the west side, became the hero of a restored community.

The voice of Ernie Harwell rang through the hot summer nights with news of another last ditch rally, another improbable comeback, another game ahead in the standings. And somehow it got better, brighter, easier.

The emotions of that season never seem to fade, because it was a time when this ballpark bridged a divided city. "My mom lost her job in 1935 because

someone gave her tickets to a Series game and she went to the ballpark instead of to work," says Carol Parker, who grew up on the east side and now lives in Petoskey.

"So when they won the Series in 1968, she felt she had to do something. So she drove home and got this tiger costume out of the closet that someone had bought her as a gag. She made me put it on and go downtown.

"I walked around for hours with that stupid thing on. But I'll never forget the joy, the look on everyone's face. We were together again and even though everyone had wanted to make that happen, no one knew how. It took the ballpark to make it real."

You could almost see this longing for community made visible in 1984. This was another time of crisis in the

city. Downtown was an empty shell with the closing of Hudson's. The auto industry had gone into the tank and no one was sure it could climb back out this time.

As layoffs mounted, despair became a dinner guest in so many homes. Once more, it was the ballpark that was a beacon.

It was the year of The Wave. It may have started in another part of the country, in some other stadium. But it was at Michigan and Trumbull that it swelled to its greatest height.

It is a tired sports cliche now. But when The Wave was new, as the Tigers started the season at 35-5 and the fever raged through this area as never before, it was a thrilling sight to watch as it made its way around the park.

From the centerfield bleachers, where it usually began, and then crashing across the packed grandstand in left, through the season ticket boxes around the infield, then out to right before completing the circle back to the bleachers for the wavemasters to start it around once more.

It was as if this city's crippled sense of community was being made whole again with this odd group ritual. The ballpark had become a source of unity, a way to share something good.

There was no way we could have known it then, but that was the zenith. In that summer of The Wave and Bless You, Boys, new attendance records and unfailing delight, the ballpark had entered its twilight.

The new, hard-eyed economics of professional sports was about to squeeze the life out of it. The implacable demographics of Metro Detroit demanded a special occasion and added comforts for the occasional fan to come downtown.

New cable TV channels made it too easy to sit at home and watch. As the team began to decline in the late 80s, fewer and fewer fans would make the effort.

The Tiger Stadium Fan Club tried gallantly, sometimes feverishly, to stave off the inevitable. It fought for years, on talk shows and columns and in the courts, to save it. It organized a group hug one spring, just to show the old park that we still cared.

But economics, as usual, trumped emotion. When a new stadium was sold to the public on the basis of revitalizing the core of downtown, there was no defense.

So now its Opening Days are over. Another large chunk of what we had thought of as a defining part of Detroit will soon pass away.

EUPHORIA REPLACED DESPAIR IN 1984 WHEN KIRK GIBSON'S HOME RUN CLINCHED THE TIGERS' FOURTH WORLD SERIES CHAMPIONSHIP.

"When I came here for the first time, with an older cousin, we sat in the bleachers," recalls Jeff Shillman, of Franklin. "This older guy must have been eavesdropping on our conversation, because just before the game started he leaned forward and tapped me on the shoulder.

"'You just keep your eyes open,' he told me, 'and you'll see some things.' I did, and he was right about that."

There will be other memories made in the new ballpark. Maybe there will be other times when the city will need it to provide the sort of spirit that calms fears and soothes the soul and brings us together.

Other children, holding tightly to the hands of a parent, will enter its gates and, just as we did, fall helplessly in love with a game and a team for the rest of their lives.

But this piece of Detroit was ours for a long, long time. And we will miss it terribly.

In the beginning

JULY 4, 1887

Before there was a Navin Field, a Briggs Stadium or a Tiger Stadium, The National
League's Detroit Wolverines played baseball at Recreation Park on the near east side
of town at the corner of Brush and Brady Streets. The team did not draw well, even after
winning the championship in 1887, and folded in 1888 after just eight seasons
in the National League.

Wildcat Tiger fans

DATE UNKNOWN

The erection of Wildcat stands by area homeowners was an ongoing problem at Bennett Park. The stands, built on tops of barns and other buildings, severely undercut the Tigers profit margin because owners would charge a fraction of what it would cost to actually get into the ballpark. Many of the stands would accommodate up to 75 fans at a time, making it a very profitable business on game day.

17

Pittsburgh Tigers?

1903

In this early action shot taken in a game in Detroit, New York Highlanders third baseman Wid Conroy leaps to catch an errant throw. By 1903 the current arrangement between the American League and National League was born, resulting in joint recognition of the two leagues and establishment of the World Series. The agreement prevented the Tigers from relocating to Pittsburgh, where they would have competed against the National League Pirates.

Can you play, kid?

1905

Ty Cobb, a tender rookie of 18, gets instruction from well-dressed manager Bill Armour.
Cobb would bat only .240 in his first season in Detroit, but never finished
lower than .320 thereafter. When his career finally ended in 1928,
Cobb would boast the highest career average (.367) in major-league history,
a mark that still stands.

The original freebie

DATE UNKNOWN

Don't have a ticket? Some Detroiters before the turn of the century got a chance to see the Tigers play anyway at Boulevard Park, the original home of the Tigers at the corner of Lafayette and Helen Streets. The wooden structure would last until 1895, when team owner George Vanderbeck purchased the land at Michigan and Trumbull and began construction of Bennett Park.

You can't catch me

1904

Ty Cobb was safe at home in this close play at the plate, sliding deftly under the tag

of Boston catcher Lou Criger in a game at Bennett Park.

Cobb had perfected a slide where he would swerve his body away from the tag at the last

moment and touch the corner of the plate

as he was going by.

A title team in waiting

1907

The Tigers first World Series team poses for a picture at Bennett Park. The Tigers played in three consecutive World Series (1907-09) but wouldn't win their first championship until 1935. Ty Cobb (second row, third from left) was only 20 in 1907, but he led the league in hitting with a .350 average. The pitching staff included three 20-game winners and an 18-gamer. Between the four, they accounted for all but four of the team's 92 victories that year.

Always the bridesmaid

1908

The 1907 American League pennant is paraded around Bennett Park before a game.
Despite a star-studded lineup that included the likes of Ty Cobb, Sam Crawford and
twenty-game winners Bill Donovan, Ed Killian and George Mullins, the Tigers would repeat
the ritual the next two years but wouldn't get an opportunity to hoist
a World Series flag until 1935.

Exhibit 'A' for the defense

AUGUST 24, 1909

Hall of Fame center fielder Ty Cobb was called a "Genius in Spikes" by Tigers fans, and a "demon in spikes" by opponents. In this play in 1909, he spiked A's Hall of Famer Frank "Home Run" Baker while sliding into third. Cobb had a reputation for sharpening his cleats and trying to injure enemy infielders. But when the Athletics accused him of deliberately injuring Baker, this photo was considered enough to disprove the claim.

A Hall of Fame photo shoot

APRIL 26, 1911

Ty Cobb tries out his photography skills on fellow Hall-of-Famer Sam Crawford in this rare shot, taken at Bennett Park. For 15 seasons, Crawford played alongside Cobb in the outfield, hit behind him and even pinch hit for him. But he was also overshadowed by Cobb, much as Gehrig was overshadowed by Ruth. Still, Crawford had a brilliant career, batting .309 with 2,961 hits and legging out 309 triples — the most in major-league history.

Happy birthday, George

DATE UNKNOWN

George Mullin is one of only eight pitchers to hurl a no-hitter at Michigan and Trumbull.
He's the only one to do it on his birthday. Mullin beat St. Louis 7-0 on July 4, 1912 at Bennett
Park to celebrate his 32nd birthday. He also collected three hits and knocked in three runs.
Earl Hamilton returned the no-hit favor on St. Louis' next visit, holding the Tigers hitless
in a 5-1 victory on August 30.

Play ball!

APRIL 20, 1912

The Tigers watch as the American flag is raised for the first time during Navin Field opening
festivities. An overflow crowd of 24,384 watched the Tigers rally past Cleveland 6-5 in
11 innings. Ty Cobb was his usual aggressive self with a steal of home after his first at-bat.
Much of the attention in the newspaper the next day was diverted by one of the world's most
famous disasters — the sinking of the Titantic.

He only acted that way

DATE UNKNOWN

Hughie Jennings, second only to Sparky Anderson in years of service as a Tigers manager, held a law degree from Cornell. Jennings was much beloved by Detroit fans for his on-the-field antics, including ringing a bell in the dugout during this game. While Jennings may have seemed a bit on the strange side, he survived in Detroit for 14 years, winning 1,131 games.

'I got it!'

APRIL 27, 1912

Sam Crawford chases a fly ball in the sun at Navin Field. Note the early form of sunglasses
Crawford is sporting. "Wahoo" Sam got his nickname from the town of Wahoo, Nebraska,
where he was born in 1880. He batted .325 in 1912, but was overshadowed by teammate
Ty Cobb and his major league-leading .410 average. Crawford is tops all-time
in triples (312) and inside-the-park home runs (51).

Eee-yaah!!

DATE UNKNOWN

That was the nickname of Hughie Jennings, who managed the Tigers
to American League pennants in 1907, 1908 and 1909, but never won a World Series.
A shortstop for the original Baltimore Orioles, Jennings managed the Tigers and coached
third base from 1907-20. He was inducted into
the Baseball Hall of Fame in 1945.

He had no equal

AUGUST 29, 1925

Among the greats who have worn a Tigers uniform, Ty Cobb stands above all others. The Sporting News recently named him the third best player of all time, behind Babe Ruth and Willie Mays. Cobb played at both Bennett Park and Navin Field during his 22-year career with the Tigers, and he appeared in three World Series, but never won one. As complete a player as he was, Cobb's number has never been retired by the Tigers — he played in an era without uniform numbers.

Tampering with the mail

DATE UNKNOWN

Two key figures in Tigers history, owner Frank Navin and Tigers star Ty Cobb,
talk on game day before the crowd starts filtering into Navin Field. When Navin found out
that Cobb was being pursued by the rival Federal League, he had Cobb's
telegrams stolen so that he could keep abreast
of the negotiations.

Fire in his belly

AUGUST 29, 1925

Although Ty Cobb was a great player, he wasn't the friendliest guy in town. Here he signs autographs for two young Tigers fans. But when it came to fellow players — including his own teammates — Cobb was known to be aloof, owner of a hair-trigger temper and a bigot. For all his personality flaws, even those who had to endure his shortcomings respected his on-the-field abilities.

No horsing around

1926

Mounted police push back the opening day crowd at Navin Field, Ty Cobb's
last year as manager of the team. The excitement of opening day was soon forgotten, and by
the halfway point of the season Cobb had replaced himself in center field
and relegated himself to coaching from the bench to avoid the boos
that rang down from the crowd.

Slow as molasses

1926

If Harry Heilmann is safe at first base, most other players probably
would have made it to second. Despite his slowness afoot, Heilmann was able to win
four batting titles. Had he possessed any sort of speed, Heilmann likely
would have batted .400 at least twice and his .342 career average
would have been considerably higher.

Hard times in Tigertown

APRIL 1928

Ground crew members till the soil at Navin Field in 1928, a down time at the corner
of Michigan and Trumbull. Late in the season, with the Tigers relegated
to a second-division finish, only 404 diehard fans showed up
for a game against Boston. It remains the Tigers smallest home crowd
since joining the American League.

Not in my house

DATE UNKNOWN

Don't let the smiles fool you — Babe Ruth and Ty Cobb didn't like each other. Cobb always
resented the way the Detroit fans warmed up to the Babe whenever he performed there.
While the fans hoped that Ruth would hit one of his legendary tape-measure home runs,
Cobb would do a slow burn as he saw his reputation
as the game's dominant player slip away.

A great Michigander

1934

Charlie Gehringer looks out at the field as he awaits his turn at bat. The Fowlerville (Mich.)
native was an all-around player who not only batted more than .300 in 13 of his 16 seasons,
but was called by Ty Cobb one of the two "greatest second basemen (he) ever saw."
Gehringer's .320 career batting average is sixth on the Tigers all-time list.
Cobb, of course, is tops at .367.

Can you sign, Mr. Goslin?

1934

Goose Goslin, who said Detroit was the best baseball town he had ever played in, signs
autographs for some young fans at Navin Field. Moments like this have kept baseball
at "The Corner" so intimate between the Tigers and their fans. Through the generations
fans remember their interaction with Tigers greats ...
and even the not-so-greats.

A rampaging rookie takes a break

AUGUST 25, 1934

Schoolboy Rowe relaxes in the dugout on the day he made his rookie year a record-setting one. He defeated the Washington Senators 4-2 for his 16th consecutive victory. He also drove in the winning run in the ninth inning. Rowe finished the year with a 24-8 record, the best of his career, and helped the Tigers make their first World Series appearance in 25 years.

He could have been a Tiger

SEPTEMBER 19, 1934

Player-manager Mickey Cochrane, on his way to leading the Tigers to two consecutive pennants, including their first World Series victory in 1935, chats with Babe Ruth at Navin Field before the Babe's final game in Detroit. Amazingly, Cochrane almost didn't get the job. Owner Frank Navin had invited Ruth to Detroit to discuss managing, but the Yankee slugger instead took his family on vacation and told Navin he'd see him later. Navin turned to Cochrane instead.

Beginning of the end

OCTOBER 3, 1934

It isn't quite the crush of media at a Super Bowl, but Tigers manager Mickey Cochrane
and St. Louis manager Frankie Frisch shake hands and accommodate journalists
and photographers before Game 1 of the World Series.
The Cardinals took Game 1 at Navin Field and went on
to win the series in seven games.

Wait until next year...

OCTOBER 5, 1934

Babe Ruth, with a little experience to back him up, gives Tigers star Hank Greenberg
a few pointers before Game 3 of the 1934 World Series. Unfortunately, the Tigers lost the game
4-1 (on an eight-hitter by Paul Dean of the Cardinals) and eventually the series, too. The Tigers
would finally break through in 1935, winning their first world baseball championship after
four unsuccessful attempts.

Public transportation

OCTOBER 8, 1934

Trolley cars were a popular source of transportation to Tigers games during the 1930s,
at least for those who could afford the fare. In this photo, hundreds of fans exit a trolley car
near the Navin Field offices at the corner of Michigan and Trumbull
before Game 6 of the 1934 World Series. The Tigers lost the game and
the series 4-3 to the St. Louis Cardinals.

Dean takes Rowe to school

OCTOBER 8, 1934

Schoolboy Rowe, who won a record 16 in a row early in the 1934 season, warms up
before Game 6 of the World Series. Rowe didn't fare as well in this game,
losing 4-3 to Paul Dean as the Cardinals tied the series.
St. Louis went on to win Game 7
to deny the Tigers their first World Series championship.

Safe at the plate

OCTOBER 8, 1934

Jack Rothrock scores on a Joe Medwick single in Game 6 of the World Series as the Cardinals take a first-inning lead. The Tigers, who had returned to Detroit leading the series 3-2 and in need of a single victory for their first championship, tied the score at 3-3 in the sixth inning, but St. Louis pitcher Paul Dean knocked in the winning run in the seventh and tossed a seven-hitter to win 4-3.

Rotten deal for Medwick

OCTOBER 9, 1934

Baseball Commissioner Kenesaw Mountain Landis orders Joe Medwick of the Cardinals to take the rest of the day off during Game 7 of the World Series. Medwick had mixed it up with the Tigers Marv Owen and after a bench-clearing brawl, fans pelted Medwick with garbage and bottles four times before Landis' move restored order. The Cardinals' Dizzy Dean won the game 11-0 behind a 17-hit attack.

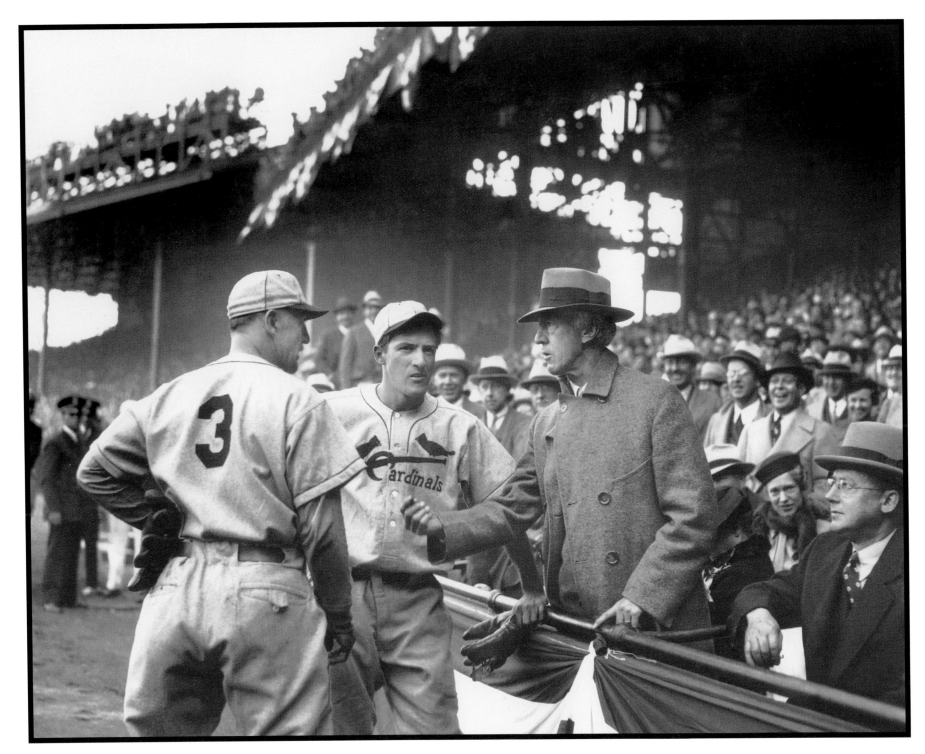

Not in Hank's house

AUGUST 30, 1935

Hank Greenberg nails a Cleveland pitch for his 30th home run of the season, an MVP year for "Hammerin' Hank." The Tigers used a home-field advantage to win the 1935 World Series, losing the opener at Navin Field but sweeping the remaining three games there to win the series 4-2 against the Chicago Cubs. Their Game 6 victory touched off a wild night of celebration in downtown Detroit.

A bird's eye view

OCTOBER 2, 1935

An aerial view shows a packed Navin Field during Game 1 of the 1935 World Series.
The shoulder-to-shoulder fans had little to celebrate during the game as the Chicago Cubs
took the opener 3-0 as Ron Warneke outpitched Schoolboy Rowe. The Tigers rebounded with
an 8-3 victory in Game 2, scoring four runs in the first inning before the Cubs managed
to retire a batter.

Tickets, tickets, who's got tickets?

OCTOBER 2, 1935

Fans line up early at Navin Field hoping to purchase remaining bleacher seats
before Game 1 of the 1935 World Series. The opener, played in Detroit because the
Chicago Cubs needed time to prepare Wrigley Field for the series, drew 47,391.
The Tigers lost the opener 3-0, but needed just six games to win their
first world championship.

Three stars of the game

OCTOBER 7, 1935

The three heroes of Game 6 of the 1935 World Series celebrate in the Tigers locker room
after the game. Tommy Bridges (right) was the winning pitcher; Goose Goslin
knocked in Mickey Cochrane with the winning run with a sinking line drive single into center
field. The two-out base hit gave the Tigers a 4-3 victory and touched off
a lot of locker room hugging.

The sky's the limit

APRIL 20, 1937

After winning their first World Series in 1935, the Tigers finished second but a distant
19.5 games behind the Yankees in 1936. Still, with the batting of Charlie Gehringer
(.371, 133 runs) and Hank Greenberg (.337, 93 extra-base hits and 183 RBI), and the pitching
of Roxie Lawson (18-7), Eldon Auker (17-9) and Tommy Bridges (15-12), the 1937 team
expected to make the Series again. Alas, the Tigers went 89-65 — 13 games behind the Yankees.

Loaded with talent

AUGUST 29, 1937

Hank Greenberg and rookie Rudy York of the Tigers pose with the Yankees' Bill Dickey
(far left), Lou Gehrig and Joe DiMaggio. Two days later York would break one of Babe
Ruth's records with 18 home runs in August when he hit two against the Washington
Senators in D.C. He finished the year with 35 home runs and
would never top that mark again.

Hats off to Rudy York

AUGUST 30, 1937

A Yankee batboy picks up hats tossed onto the playing field at Navin Field after a Rudy York home run. It was a tradition on Labor Day for the men to sail their hats onto the field at the first positive thing the Tigers did during the game. In Ty Cobb's day, he would have groundskeepers pick them up and he would take them back to his farm in Georgia and put them on the heads of his donkeys to keep them out of the sun.

He wore out his welcome

AUGUST 7, 1938

Mickey Cochrane talks with Boston's Joe Cronin after the Tigers manager-general manager was fired following a second consecutive home loss to the Red Sox. By then the glow was off new Briggs Stadium, with Cochrane being second guessed by anyone with an ounce of baseball knowledge. The line on his 4^1/$_2$ years in Detroit: 2 pennants, 2 second-place finishes and the team's first World Series title.

Monkey suits

1938

Briggs Stadium vendors model their uniforms and show off their wares before a game. When the Tigers were owned by Frank Navin and then Walter Briggs, every ballpark employee was expected to dress accordingly. This policy included everyone from vendors, to ticket takers, to cigarette girls to the ground crew. And although the uniforms changed over the years, the intention was always to provide a pleasant atmosphere at the ballpark.

Man for all positions

JUNE 12, 1939

Rudy York, better known for his bat than his glove, makes a catch in foul territory. In fact, the
Tigers bounced him around just to keep his potent bat in the starting lineup. In 1937, he replaced
an injured Mickey Cochrane behind the plate and responded with 35 homers and 103 RBI. In
1940, Hank Greenberg was moved from first base to left field to make way for York, who batted
.316 with 33 home runs and 134 RBI. York also played the outfield and third base for Detroit.

Louis comes home a champ

SEPTEMBER 20, 1939

Although baseball has been king at "The Corner," the site has also held other significant events.
Here hometown favorite Joe Louis throws the 11th-round punch that
knocked out Bob Pastor, a victory in keeping with Detroit's reputation as City of Champions.
The fight was scheduled for 20 rounds, with the ring set up in the middle
of the Briggs Stadium infield.

Birthday boy

MAY 11, 1940

Charlie Gehringer gets the star treatment from newspaper photographers and other members of the media on his 37th birthday. Gehringer, always a favorite because of his Michigan ties (he was born in Fowlerville), was taken aback when the ushers rolled out a giant birthday cake onto the Briggs Stadium field. Despite his advancing age, Gehringer still managed to hit .313 for the 1940 American League champions.

Both sides of the pitch

AUGUST 3, 1940

Schoolboy Rowe revs up to fire one to the plate in a game at Briggs Stadium.
Rowe pitched for the Tigers for parts of nine seasons. Not only was he a capable pitcher,
he was also pretty good with the bat. In one game in 1935 he had a double, a triple,
3 singles and 3 RBI. For his career Rowe batted .263 and
knocked in 153 runs.

Friends and family

OCTOBER 6, 1940

Tiger Stadium has always been a place of unity for Detroiters, a place where they could put
aside their differences and share a game of baseball. No matter how bad things seemed
to get elsewhere, baseball at the "The Corner" was always a pleasant diversion
for young and old fans alike, especially at a game such as Game 5
of the 1940 World Series.

His heart was in it, but...

AUGUST 27, 1944

Rookie Hal Newhouser and retired Tigers great Charlie Gehringer, now in the military, meet in the locker room at Briggs Stadium. Newhouser had intended to join the service to fight for his country during World War II, and was to take his oath on the Briggs Stadium mound before a game. However, a heart murmur was detected during his physical so he remained with the Tigers.

Never skipped a beat

SEPTEMBER 26, 1946

With the center field bleachers as a backdrop, Hank Greenberg rounds third base after hitting his 43rd home run of the season. Greenberg led the majors with 44 home runs and topped the American League with 127 RBI. Greenberg — then in his first full year after returning from a four-year stint in the army — hit a grand slam in his first game back with the Tigers in July 1945.

Tigers turn on the switch

JUNE 15, 1948

The lights finally go on at Briggs Stadium, the last American League ballpark to host
a night game. A crowd of 54,480 turned out to watch the Tigers play the Philadelphia
Athletics. The A's hitters must have had trouble picking up the ball in the light provided
by the new $40,000 system as Hal Newhouser tossed a two-hitter
in a 4-1 victory by the Tigers.

Silence for a silenced star

JULY 10, 1951

The American League team pauses for a moment to honor former Tigers great Harry Heilmann prior to the 1951 All-Star game at Briggs Stadium. Heilmann, inducted into the Hall of Fame in 1952, died the day before the game in Southfield (Mich.) at age 56. The righthander batted .390 or better four times, including .403 in 1923. Heilmann was the voice of the Tigers on radio for 17 years beginning in 1934.

Alone in his thoughts

1952

Tigers general manager Charlie Gehringer sits among the empty seats at Briggs Stadium
during a loss to the New York Yankees. The 1952 season was one of the worst years in
team history, with the Tigers finishing in last place for the first time
with a 50-104 record, even though 32 of those victories came at home.
On July 4, manager Red Rolfe was fired.

SECTION 32 SECTION 32

115

A long-time Tiger

MAY 1957

Al Kaline takes batting practice at an empty Briggs Stadium.
In 1980 Kaline became only the 10th player to be elected to the Baseball Hall of Fame
in his first attempt. When he retired he became only the second Tigers player — Ty Cobb
was the other — to play more than 20 seasons
in a Detroit uniform.

The other cats at 'The Corner'

DECEMBER 18, 1957

The Tigers weren't the only tenants at Tiger Stadium. The Detroit Lions also called the stadium home from 1938 through 1974. The team won their last championship there as the Lions defeated the Cleveland Browns 59-14 behind quarterback Kyle Rote's four touchdown passes and one run for a score. The Lions also won their first championship at Tiger Stadium, again against the Browns in 1953.

Colorful debut for Virgil

JUNE 15, 1958

Although Ozzie Virgil gets the label "first black player" for the Tigers, the truth was that even Virgil didn't consider himself black; he was born in the Dominican Republic. Walter Briggs chose Virgil because of his light coloring. Nonetheless, Virgil's opening-day performance at Briggs Stadium was a keeper when he went 5-for-5 against the Washington Senators.

All-Star voices

SEPTEMBER 1961

George Kell (center) and Ernie Harwell call a game from the booth at Tiger Stadium, with engineer Howard Stitzel in the background. Kell retired after the 1996 season, but Harwell has called Tigers games every year since 1960 season except 1992. The Tigers have had great radio and television voices over the years, going back as far as Ty Tyson, the original voice of the Tigers, who called games for WWJ from 1927-42.

Back in uniform

JUNE 1, 1964

Al Kaline of the Tigers and former Cardinals great Stan Musial talk in the batting cage at Tiger Stadium before an exhibition game between the two teams. Musial, inducted into the Baseball Hall of Fame in 1969, had retired the year before but suited up for the love of the game. Four years later, Kaline would lead the Tigers to their first World Series victory in 23 seasons, batting .379 against those same St. Louis Cardinals.

A very exclusive club

SEPTEMBER 14, 1968

Denny McLain and Dizzy Dean (in white hat) head for the dugout as the delirious Tiger Stadium crowd cheers McLain's 30th victory of the season. Dean had previously been the last man to record 30 victories back in 1934. The Tigers helped McLain to his historic victory by rallying for two runs in the ninth inning. For the season, McLain was 31-6 with a 1.96 ERA.

Here comes momentum

OCTOBER 7, 1968

Bill Freehan applies the tag that turned the World Series in the Tigers favor. The Cardinals won three of the first four games and the Tigers needed a home victory to remain alive. With the Cardinals up 3-2 in the fifth, Lou Brock attempted to score on a single and was gunned down by Willie Horton. Al Kaline singled home two runs in the seventh to win it 5-3, and the Tigers would go on to win the next two games in St. Louis to clinch the title.

Tigertown tough guys

1969

Willie Horton (left) and Gates Brown were two of the first black fan favorites to play
for the Tigers. Horton, one of sixteen kids raised in a Detroit housing project, hit 262 home
runs during his career with Detroit and was one of the most feared long-ball hitters in the
American League. Brown, who was nicknamed so because of time spent in prison, was one of
the most accomplished pinch-hitters in baseball history.

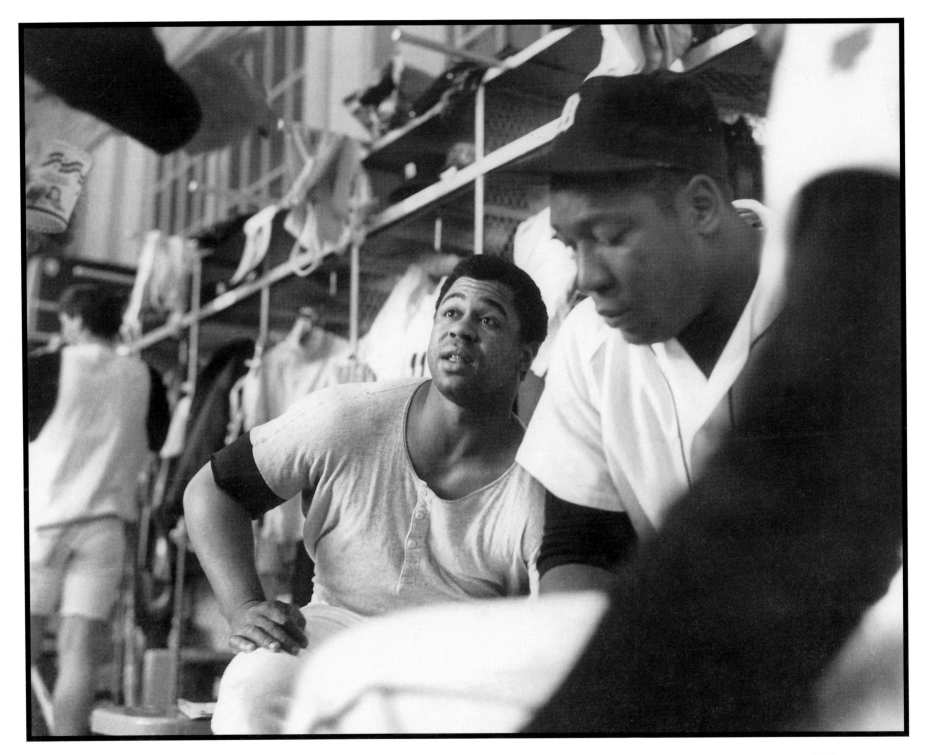

Lights out for Reggie

JULY 13, 1971

Only the light tower got in the way of Reggie Jackson's mammoth pinch hit home run in the 1971 All-Star Game at Tiger Stadium. It would have cleared the roof and landed on Trumbull Avenue had it not struck the light tower on the way up. The ball hit the steel base of the tower and bounced away. Jackson's home run off Pittsburgh's Doc Ellis ignited the American League, which won the game for the first time since 1962.

Base brawl comes to town

AUGUST 22, 1972

Tigers manager Billy Martin — the inventor of a fiery brand of baseball called Billy Ball — had the last word this day after a brawl erupted between the Tigers and the Oakland Athletics. But the A's would get the ultimate last word when they beat the Tigers in the American League Championship Series to advance to the World Series. Martin eventually wore out his welcome and he was fired late in the 1973 season.

The one-year wonder

JUNE 28, 1976

For one season Mark "The Bird" Fidrych captivated the baseball world like few players ever have. The gangly rookie's youthful enthusiasm made him the No. 1 box-office attraction in 1976. No matter where he pitched crowds of up to 40,000 fans could be expected. Fidrych posted a 19-9 record and led the American League with a 2.34 ERA. However, injuries kept him from pitching another full season, and he was only 10-10 over the next four years before retiring.

A new wave Tiger

OCTOBER 14, 1984

This unusual perspective of Kirk Gibson's historic home run off the Padres' Goose Gossage in the deciding game of the 1984 World Series shows how fans reacted moments after the ball took flight. Gibson, who has two of the most memorable home runs in World Series history, crushed the Gossage fastball deep into the right-field upper deck. He then showed his flair for the theatrical by rounding the bases, pumping his fists and blowing kisses to the Tiger Stadium crowd.

It was a marvelous season

OCTOBER 14, 1984

Catcher Lance Parrish (left) and reliever Willie Hernandez leap for joy after Hernandez recorded the final out in Game 5 of the 1984 World Series. Hernandez's splendid season was one of the many reasons the Tigers got off to a 35-5 record and won 104 games. He recorded 32 saves, had a 1.92 ERA and was rewarded by being named both the American League's MVP and Cy Young Award winner.

Hometown hero wins it

OCTOBER 4, 1987

Frank Tanana, a Catholic Central product, celebrates with Tigers second baseman
Lou Whitaker after Tanana defeated Toronto 1-0 at Tiger Stadium to clinch the American
League East division title. Detroit topped the majors with 98 victories and 225 home runs, but
fell to the eventual World Series champion Minnesota Twins in the American League
Championship Series, losing in five games.

Rallying behind Mandela

JUNE 28, 1990

Tiger Stadium has been the site of many political gatherings during its history, including a 1990 rally where 49,000 people filled the stadium to hear South African leader Nelson Mandela speak on the issue of apartheid in South Africa, shortly after Mandela was released from jail where he served time as a political prisoner. Many of Metro Detroit's prominent African American citizens — including Aretha Franklin — attended the event.

Hit it here, Cecil

SEPTEMBER 26, 1990

Seven-year old Brent Mees came all the way from Jackson to watch Cecil Fielder's attempt
to hit 50 home runs. With his father's glove slipping out of his tiny hand, he waited,
and waited, and waited ... But Fielder wouldn't break the 50-homer barrier until
the final game of the season in New York. For good measure, Fielder hit another shot and
finished with 51.

More than just a job

SEPTEMBER 30, 1992

Joseph Direbk, a Tiger Stadium guard for 10 years, sits in a tunnel at the stadium
trying to keep his hands warm as temperatures drop throughout the Tigers final home
game of the 1992 season. While Tiger Stadium is made of cold stone and steel,
the old structure has warmed the hearts of many of its employees,
some of whom have worked there for over 30 years.

Fielder on the roof

JULY 22, 1993

Cecil Fielder takes to the roof at Tiger Stadium for a smoke and a little batting practice.
Actually, Fielder just wanted to see where his monster home run had landed a month before.
He had just won the IBM Tale of the Tape award for longest home run in the month of June,
a regular occurrence for the first baseman. Cecil's blast — hit on June 24 — traveled
475 feet and landed on the left-field roof.

Gray-haired greatness

SEPTEMBER 13, 1995

Manager Sparky Anderson looks like he's waiting out the end in Detroit. But in his years
at the helm in Detroit, Anderson won more games than any Tigers manager with 1,331.
On the all-time list he ranks second with 2,194 victories. He's the only manager to hold career
records with two different teams, to record 100-victory seasons in both leagues and
to manage teams in both leagues to World Series championships.

A capable combination

SEPTEMBER 13, 1995

Alan Trammell and Lou Whitaker, appearing before a disappointing Tiger Stadium crowd, acknowledge the few fans who showed up to see them break the league record for games played together as teammates. Over 19 years the shortstop-second baseman combination had played in 1,915 games, breaking the record set by George Brett and Frank White of the Kansas City Royals.

Ghost of Rudy York

JUNE 25, 1998

Thanks to interleague play, fans get to see a record fall at Tiger Stadium. The Cubs' Sammy Sosa hit his 19th home run of the month off Brian Moehler to topple the 51-year-old mark set by the Tigers' Rudy York in 1937. Sosa, the 1998 National League MVP, finished the month with 20 homers. He would battle the Cardinals' Mark McGwire to the wire in the most prolific home-run race in baseball history. McGwire finished with 70, Sosa with 66.

The last time

APRIL 12, 1999

Willie Blair throws the first pitch at 1:04 p.m. on the final opening day at Tiger Stadium.
A sellout crowd saw the Tigers lose 1-0 in extra innings, but by the time the story is through
being told, just about every Metro Detroiter will claim to have been in attendance.
Next year's opener will be another historic occasion — the first year
of Comerica Park.

ACKNOWLEDGEMENT

Our thanks

Our memories of the ballpark on "The Corner" are more vividly enhanced by the photographs in this book. Whether it be Bennett Park, Navin Field, Briggs Stadium or Tiger Stadium, Detroit News photographers have recorded images that will remain forever.

Early photographs were not attributed, keeping us from giving proper credit to each picture. However, we can acknowledge those staff photographers whose work does appear in this book. They include: William Kuenzel, Monroe D. Stroecker, Milton Brooks, William Seiter, Rolland Ransom, Don Walker, James Kilpatrick, Peter A. MacGregor, Edwin C. Lombardo, Drayton Holcomb, Duane Belanger, William T. Anderson, Diane Weiss, Michael S. Green, Joe DeVera, David C. Coates, Dale G. Young, Steve Perez and Steve Fecht.

ON OUR COVER: OCTOBER 9, 1934. TIGER FANS STORM THE INFIELD AND HOIST HOME PLATE AT NAVIN FIELD AFTER LOSING, 11-0, TO THE ST. LOUIS CARDINALS IN GAME 7 OF THE WORLD SERIES. THEY COULD NOT HAVE KNOWN THAT A YEAR LATER THEIR HEROES WOULD WIN IT ALL — 4 GAMES TO 2 — AGAINST THE CHICAGO CUBS FOR THEIR FIRST WORLD CHAMPIONSHIP.